D1709770

PECOS BILL

and

LIGHTNING

By LEIGH PECK

Illustrated by

KURT WIESE

WITHDRAWN FROM
J. EUGENE SMITH LIBRARY
EASTERN CONN STATE COLLEGE
Eastern Conn State College
WILLIMANTIC, CT 06226
Willimantic, Conn. 06226

F. R. Noble School Library

HOUGHTON MIFFLIN COMPANY · BOSTON

The Riverside Press Cambridge

1940

CHILDREN'S LIBRARY
Windham Street School
Willimantic, Conn.

THE STORIES

COPYRIGHT, 1940, BY LEIGH PECK

ALL RIGHTS RESERVED INCLUDING THE RIGHT TO REPRODUCE
THIS BOOK OR PARTS THEREOF IN ANY FORM

PRINTED IN THE U.S.A.

CHILDREN'S LIBRARY
Windham Street School
Willimantic, Conn.

8.2

HOW PECOS BILL BEGAN

EVERYWHERE and at all times men have worked hard and tried to do their best, but sometimes have failed. Then they have comforted themselves for their failures by making up stories of a hero, a man like themselves, but able to do all the things they wanted to do and could not. The Greeks, long ago, told stories of Odysseus and of Prometheus. The Saxons called their hero Beowulf.

The men that work in the North Woods of our country call him Paul Bunyan. Their hero is a giant whose voice roars like the thunder and whose step shakes the ground like an earthquake.

The ranch men of the Southwest call him Pecos Bill. He is no giant like Paul Bunyan, but he is as strong and brave as any hero that men have ever dreamed of any-where. Of all the heroes, he is the gayest. He tosses a jest no less lightly than he tosses his lariat, and he laughs in the face of death itself.

I

13828

F. R. Noble School Library
Eastern Conn. State College
Willimantic, Conn.   06226

CHILDREN'S LIBRARY
Windham Street School
Willimantic, Conn.

When cowboys sit by their campfires at night, they like to tell each other stories about Pecos Bill. They say that he has done all the things that they would like to do. He is what all the real cowboys would like to be. No matter how tired and worried they are, they feel better after they have told each other the brave deeds of Pecos Bill.

There is a reason why they call their hero 'Pecos' Bill. To call him 'Pecos' Bill is to say that he is 'plenty good' and 'plenty tough,' because the land along the Pecos River is a very rough ranching country, and many cattle thieves and warlike Indians used to live there. A cowboy had to be 'plenty good' and 'plenty tough' to run cattle along the Pecos River. Pecos Bill was so good that he could ride the lightning, and so tough that the cyclones learned to keep out of his way.

Here are some of the stories that the cowboys tell each other about their hero, Pecos Bill.

2

PECOS BILL'S YOUTH

No WONDER Pecos Bill was so brave. His mother was a very brave woman. One morning before breakfast she swept forty-five Indian chiefs out of her yard with her broom.

When Davy Crockett heard how brave she was, he sent her a Bowie knife as a present. All her eighteen children cut their teeth on that Bowie knife.

Her nearest neighbor lived one hundred miles away. When one day she heard that a new neighbor had moved in only fifty miles away, she decided, 'This part of Texas is getting too crowded. We must move out where we will have more room.'

So Pecos Bill's father hitched the old spotted cow and the old red mule to the old covered wagon. The father and mother put their eighteen children into the wagon, and they started out over the prairie. Their son Bill was four years old then. He sat in the very end of the wagon, with his feet hanging out.

When they were driving through the low waters of the Pecos River, one wheel of the wagon hit a rock, and the jolt threw Bill right out of the wagon and into the sand of the river. No one saw him fall or heard him call, 'Wait for me!'

After Bill saw that the wagon was going on without him, he got up and ran after it. But his short little legs could not go so fast as the wagon. Soon it was gone, and Bill was left all alone.

There were still seventeen children in the wagon, and no one noticed that little Bill was gone, until his mother counted the children at dinner time.

'Where is Bill?' she asked.

No one had seen him since they crossed the river. So the family hurried back to the river and hunted for little Bill. They looked and looked, but they could not find him. Because they had lost him at the Pecos River, they always spoke of him after that as their little lost Pecos Bill.

Little Pecos Bill was not lost long. His father and mother never did find him, but he was found by an old grandfather Coyote, named Grampy.

Grampy showed little Pecos Bill berries to eat, dug up

4

roots for him, and found mesquite beans for him, too. At night Grampy led Pecos Bill to his cave in the mountain where he could sleep safe and warm.

Grampy showed his man-child to each of the other hunting animals, and asked them not to hurt little Pecos Bill. The Bear grunted, 'W-f-f-f! I will not hurt your man-child. I will show him where to find wild honey in the bee trees.'

The Wolf yelped, 'I will not hurt your man-child. Let him come play with my cubs.'

The Polecat purred, 'I will not hurt your man-child if he will promise not to pull my lovely long tail. I will not put any of my perfume on him.'

But the Rattlesnake shook his rattles, 'Th-r-r-r!' and hissed, 'S-s-s-s! Keep him out of my way! I bite anybody that crosses my path, but I give fair warning first. Th-r-r-r! S-s-s-s!'

The Mountain Lion yowled, 'Get your child out of my way before I eat him up! A nice fat man-child is what I like to eat best of all!'

So all the hunting animals except the Rattlesnake and the Mountain Lion promised to be good to little Pecos Bill. He learned to talk to all the animals and birds in their own languages.

But the Coyotes liked Pecos Bill best of all. They taught him how to hunt. When he grew older, he was

able to run so fast that he could catch the long-eared Jack Rabbit and the long-tailed Road-Runner. Finally he grew big enough to catch the Deer, and even the Antelope, which runs fastest of any animal. He grew strong enough to pull down a Buffalo for his brother Coyotes. He climbed the mountain-tops and jumped about from crag to crag to catch the Mountain Sheep.

When one of the Coyotes got a cactus thorn in his foot or a porcupine quill in his nose, Pecos Bill pulled it out. The Coyotes were all very proud of their brother and

very fond of him.   At night he went out on the prairie
with the Coyotes and howled at the moon.   He thought
he was a Coyote.

PECOS BILL BECOMES
A COWBOY

IN ALL the years while Pecos Bill was living
with the Coyotes, he had never seen a human being.
Then one day, Bill's brother Chuck came riding along on
his cowpony and found Bill. Bill was a tall young man
now, his skin was a dark brown color, and his black hair
hung long and tangled. But Chuck knew him at once,
and cried, 'Why, you are my long-lost brother, Pecos
Bill!'

Even though Pecos Bill had learned all the animal and
bird languages, he could still talk to people, too. He
said, 'I'm not your brother! I am the brother of the
Coyotes. Why, I even have fleas!'

But Chuck said, 'That doesn't prove you are a Coyote.
Why, all cowboys have a few fleas!'

'But I howl at the moon at night,' Bill insisted, and he sang a little song,

> I'm wild and woolly and full of fleas
> And never been curried below the knees,
> And this is my night to howl —
> Yippe-e-e-e!

Chuck repeated, 'That doesn't prove a thing. All cowboys howl sometimes!' Then he added: 'If you were a Coyote, you would have a tail. Look in the spring with me here, and see yourself and me in the water. See, you have no tail! You are no brother of the Coyotes — you are my brother, for you look like me.'

Bill looked at himself and Chuck in the water, and agreed, 'We do look alike, and it is true that I have no tail. Perhaps I am your brother!'

Chuck said: 'Brother, you must put on some clothes and come with me to the ranch where I work and be a cowboy too. But I don't have any extra clothes with me. I don't know what we can do!'

Pecos Bill laughed. 'If anything has to be done, I can do it! Just wait a minute, and I'll have some clothes!'

He looked around until he found a big old steer with horns measuring six feet from tip to tip. He grabbed it by the tail, yelled loudly, and scared it so badly that it

9

jumped clear out of its skin! (That didn't hurt the old steer; it wanted to grow a new hide anyhow.) From the hide Pecos Bill made himself a leather jacket, using a yucca thorn for a needle. He made some boots, too. Then he made himself a pair of leather pants, the kind that are now called chaps. Other cowboys wear them now, to keep from getting scratched when riding through thorny bushes. They learned that from Pecos Bill.

When Bill had put on his clothes, Chuck told him, 'Get up behind me on my cowpony, and he will carry both of us to the ranch.'

But Pecos Bill laughed. 'Ride your pony, and I'll go afoot, and I'll beat you to the ranch.'

Sure enough, Bill galloped along easily, faster than Chuck's cowpony could run.

Chuck argued, though: 'You really must not go up to the ranch on foot. Nobody walks in the ranch country. We must find you some old pony to ride and a quirt to whip him along with.'

Just then Pecos Bill nearly stepped on the Rattlesnake that lay in the trail. It was fifteen feet long, and had thirty rattles on the end of its tail.

'Get out of my way,' hissed Pecos Bill in snake language.

'I won't,' the Snake hissed back. 'I told Grampy long ago to teach you to stay out of my way.'

The Snake spit poison at Pecos Bill, hitting him right between the eyes. Bill said, 'I'll give you three chances at me, before I even begin to fight.'

The three shots of poison didn't even blister Pecos

11

Bill's skin. Next, Bill spit back at the Snake, right on top of the Snake's head, and the Snake fell over, unable to move for a moment.

Bill jumped on the Snake and stamped it before it had time to bite him. He caught the Snake up by the throat and asked, 'Had enough yet?'

The Snake cried, 'I give up!' Pecos Bill wrapped it around his arm and galloped on ahead of Chuck's pony.

Soon they met the Mountain Lion. He was the largest Mountain Lion in all the world, twice as large as Chuck's cowpony. The Mountain Lion growled, 'I said I would eat you up if ever you got in my way, and now I will!'

He jumped at Pecos Bill, but Bill dodged and pulled out a handful of the Mountain Lion's fur as he went by. The fight lasted for two hours. Every time the Mountain Lion tried to jump on Pecos Bill, Bill pulled out some more of his hair. The sky was so full of the Mountain Lion's hair that it was almost as dark as night. Finally the Lion lost all of his hair except just a little on the tips of his ears and under his chin. Then he begged, 'Please, Pecos Bill, will you not hurt me any more?'

'Very well,' agreed Pecos Bill, 'but you must let me ride you for a cowpony.'

So Pecos Bill jumped on the Mountain Lion's back,

and using the Rattlesnake for a quirt to whip him along with, rode on to the ranch with Chuck.

Just at sundown, Pecos Bill rode up to the cowboys' camp on the Mountain Lion, twice as big as a cowpony, and he was still using the Rattlesnake fifteen feet long for a quirt. The cowboys around the campfire were too surprised to say a word. Chuck announced proudly, 'Boys, this is my brother, Pecos Bill.'

The cowboys' supper was cooking over the campfire — a big kettle of beans and a big pot of coffee, both boiling hot. Pecos Bill stuck his hands into the boiling bean kettle, pulled out a double handful of beans, and stuck them in his mouth. He washed them down with boiling coffee, lifting the big coffee pot from the fire, and swallowing down a gallon. He wiped his mouth on a prickly pear leaf.

Then he asked, 'Who is the boss here?'

A big man seven feet tall and wearing three guns stepped forward. 'I was,' he said, 'but you are now, Pecos Bill. Anybody that can ride a Mountain Lion and use a Rattlesnake for a quirt is boss here as long as he wants to be.'

Pecos Bill found that all the cowboys had queer nick-

names. Bill's brother was called Chuck or Chuckwagon
because he was always hungry and going to the chuckwagon for something to eat. (The chuckwagon is the

cowboys' kitchen on wheels, where their food is carried when they are away from the ranch house, working with the cattle.)

The cook was a big, fat man called Beans, because he cooked so many beans for the cowboys. He cooked lots of fried cakes, or flapjacks, for them too. When a panful of flapjacks was ready to turn over, so they could cook on the other side, he tossed them all up fifty feet in the air, and they always came down right in the pan again. He often had two panfuls in the air at once.

Three-Gun Gibbs carried three pistols, one hanging from his belt over each hip, and one strapped under his arm, underneath his clothes. He just stuck his arm into the front of his shirt when he wanted to pull out that gun. Slim Morgan was so thin that he did not make any shadow at all, even with his back to the sun. Music Mouth could play two mouth-organs at the same time, his mouth was so big. All the cowboys were bow-legged, but the one called Bull Frog had legs curved like a frog's. Dude Hopkins was all dressed up in a ten-gallon hat, a belt decorated with silver dollars, and boots even higher-heeled than the other cowboys wore.

15

PECOS BILL CAPTURES THE PACING WHITE MUSTANG

Pecos bill soon got tired of riding the Mountain Lion. It did not make a very good cowpony because all the cattle were afraid of it. So Pecos Bill decided to get a real cowpony, and he asked the cowboys, 'What's the very best horse in these parts?'

They answered: 'The best horse in all the world is running loose in these very hills. He runs fast as the lightning, so we call him Lightning. Others call him the Pacing White Mustang, and some even say that his real name is Pegasus. We have all tried hard to catch him, but no one has ever got close enough to him to put a rope on him or even to see him clearly. We have chased him for days, riding our very best ponies and changing horses every two hours, but he outran all our best ponies put together.'

16

But Pecos Bill told them: 'I'll not ride a cowpony when I chase this horse. I can run faster myself than any of your ponies can.'

So Pecos Bill threw his saddle and bridle over his shoulder and set out on foot to look for the famous wild white horse. When he got close enough to take a good look at Lightning, he saw that only the horse's mane and tail were a pure white. The beautiful animal was really a light cream or pale gold color — the color of lightning itself. The Spanish people in the Southwest call such a

horse a *palomino*. He chased Lightning five days and four nights, all the way from Mexico across Texas and New Mexico and Arizona and Utah and Colorado and Wyoming and Montana, clear up to Canada, and then down to Mexico again. Pecos Bill had to throw away his saddle and bridle, as they leaped across cactus-covered plains, down steep cliffs, and across canyons.

Finally Lightning got tired of running from Pecos Bill and stopped and snorted. 'Very well, I'll let you try to ride me if you think you can! Say your prayers and jump on!'

Pecos Bill smiled. 'I say my prayers every night and every morning.' And he jumped on Lightning's back, gripping the horse's ribs with his knees and clutching the mane with his hands.

First, Lightning tried to run out from under Pecos Bill. He ran ten miles in twenty seconds! Next he jumped a mile forward and two miles backward. Then he jumped so high in the air that Pecos Bill's head was up among the stars. Next Lightning tried to push Pecos Bill off his back by running through clumps of mesquite trees. The thorns tore poor Pecos Bill's face, and left his skin torn and bleeding.

When that failed, too, Lightning reared up on his hind legs and threw himself over backward. But Pecos Bill jumped off quickly, and before Lightning could get on his feet again, Bill sat down on his shoulders and held him firmly on the ground.

'Lightning,' Pecos Bill explained, 'you are the best horse in all the world, and I am the best cowboy in all the world. If you'll let me ride you, we will become famous together, and cowboys everywhere forever and forever will praise the deeds of Pecos Bill and Lightning.'

Then Pecos Bill turned Lightning loose and told him, 'You may decide. You are free to go or to stay with me.'

The beautiful horse put his nose in Pecos Bill's hand, and said, 'I want to stay with you and be your cow-pony — the greatest cowpony in all the world.'

Pecos Bill and Lightning went back and found the saddle and bridle where Bill had thrown them. Lightning let Pecos Bill put the saddle on him, but he didn't want to take the bit of the bridle into his mouth. So Pecos Bill just put a halter on him, and guided him by pressure of the knees and by pulling on the reins of the halter.

Lightning would not let anybody but Pecos Bill ride him. Three-Gun Gibbs tried once, while Pecos Bill was not looking, but Lightning threw him so hard that he cracked the ground open where he fell. After that, the cowboys used to call Lightning 'Widow-Maker.'

PECOS BILL INVENTS
THE LARIAT AND
THE BRANDING IRON

Pecos bill was always thinking up new and better ways to do things. He invented the rawhide lariat. This is how he made it. First he found an old steer with a very tough hide. Then he grabbed the steer's tail and shouted very loudly, so as to make it jump out of its skin. He cut the steer's hide into strips and out of these made his long rawhide lariat.

The other cowboys learned to use lariats too. A cow-

boy would send his pony at full gallop after a cow, whirl his lariat above his head three or four times, and throw it over the neck of the cow when it was still ten or twenty feet away.

But no one else could throw the lariat as far as Pecos Bill could. He could throw his lariat high up in the air around the neck of a hawk or eagle in full flight, and pull it down to earth. He could rope a whole herd of cattle at once when he wanted to, throwing his lariat around a thousand cattle all at the same time. When he wanted water for his cattle during a dry spell, he just threw his lariat over a mile or two of the Rio Grande. Riding Lightning at full speed, he pulled it behind him until he got it to the tank where his cattle drank. The Southwest part of Texas is still very dry, because Pecos Bill pulled so much water out of the Rio Grande.

21

CHILDREN'S LIBRARY
Windham Street School
Willimantic, Conn.

F. R. Noble School Library
Eastern Conn. State College
Willimantic, Conn. 06226

Once Pecos Bill roped a cyclone. One hot, dry, still afternoon, he looked out and saw a funnel-shaped black cloud moving down on the ranch, with a high wind sweeping everything before it. He cried, 'The only way to save the ranch is to lasso that cyclone.'

The other cowboys shouted, 'Stop! Even Pecos Bill can't rope a cyclone!'

But Pecos Bill rode to meet it, whirling his lariat above his head. He threw the lariat right around the middle of the cloud, and pulled it down to earth, where it turned to rain.

Pecos Bill's best throw with his lariat, though, was made the time he pulled the dog star Sirius right down out of the sky to be his dog. Even Pecos Bill couldn't stand just flatfooted and throw his lariat up among the stars. First he had to get up on something high. So one day when there was a thunderstorm he watched until he saw a bolt of lightning headed right for the top of Pike's Peak. He jumped on that bolt of lightning and rode it to the mountain, jumping off just before it struck. Once he was on top of Pike's Peak, Pecos Bill did not have any trouble at all in throwing his lariat over the dog star and pulling it down. Then, when he saw another bolt of lightning going down the mountain, he just stuck

Sirius under his arm, jumped on the lightning, and rode it safely down to his own ranch.

It was Pecos Bill who taught the cowboys how to brand cattle, and Sirius helped him. Until then, there had been no way to tell which cattle belonged on one ranch and which ones belonged on some other ranch. Some way of marking them was badly needed, because the cattle did not stay on their home range. The range was not fenced, and the cattle often wandered many, many miles away from their owners' ranches. Pecos Bill saw that he must find some way to mark the cattle. He bent an iron bar until one end of it was shaped like the letters PB, but with the P turned backward and joined to the B, thus: ꟼB. The rest of the rod served as a handle. Holding it by the handle, Pecos Bill heated the lettering end of the rod in the fire until it was red-hot. Then he pointed out to Sirius the steer that he wanted to brand. Sirius chased it up to the fire where Pecos Bill was heating the branding iron. Then he leaped up, grabbed its nose between his strong jaws, and threw it to the ground. While Sirius held the steer to the ground, Pecos Bill quickly thrust the red-hot iron against the steer's hide. It burned away the animal's hair, leaving on the hide the mark ꟼB.

This brand is read by cattle men as the Crazy PB brand, as letters turned backward are called crazy. Be-

23

cause the cattle on the ranch were branded in that way, people called the ranch the Crazy PB Ranch, and spoke of the cowboys on the ranch as the Crazy PB outfit.

Pecos Bill taught his neighbors how to brand cattle, too. Each man chose a different brand. Every spring after that they held a roundup of the young cattle that were to be branded. The cowboys went out on the range, hunted up all the cows and calves, and branded each calf with whatever brand the mother was wearing. If the mother was a Crazy PB cow, then her calf belonged to the Crazy PB Ranch, and was branded with the ranch brand.

Cowboys from several different ranches would work together until all the cattle in their part of the country were branded. The cowboys learned to bull-dog steers nearly as well as Sirius could. A cowboy would ride up close to a running steer, jump from his galloping horse, and grab the steer by the horns. Then he would throw

the steer to the ground, holding it by the tail and one
horn, while another cowboy branded it. This was only
a stunt to show off, however. In ordinary ranch work, a
cowboy roped the steer he was going to brand.

PECOS BILL MEETS PAUL BUNYAN AND STARTS A NEW RANCH

Even though Pecos Bill was boss of all the cow-hands on the ranch, and had the very finest horse in all the world to ride, and had invented so many new things, he was not satisfied. He wanted to start a new ranch. A small place of just a few hundred thousand acres would do to begin with, he thought. Whenever he had a little time to spare, he rode out on Lightning looking for a good place to start a ranch. In those days, there was plenty of land that anyone could have simply by claiming it. But Pecos Bill did not want just an ordinary ranch. He wanted the very best ranch in all the world.

Finally in Arizona he found the very piece of land that he was looking for, with grass taller than a man's head for the cattle to fatten on, creeks fed by springs of pure water for them to drink, and a few trees along the banks of the creeks, for shade in the heat of the day. The land was level except for one mountain. This mountain was tall and quite steep near the top. A very queer kind of birds, seen nowhere else in the world, made their nests among the rocks on the upper slopes of the mountain. They had to lay square-shaped eggs, because round eggs would have rolled right down the mountain.

Pecos Bill thought that this mountain would be just right for his headquarters ranch. The cattle could always find on it the climate they liked best. In cold days they could graze at the foot of the mountain, but in hot weather they could move up near the top, where it would always be cool. They could even have sunshine or shade, just as they wished, for one side of the mountain would be sunny while the other side was in the shade. It would not be likely to rain on both sides of the mountain at once, either, so the cattle could almost always keep dry. Certainly, the wind could not blow from more than one direction at once, and the cattle could always find a sheltered place where the wind was not blowing on them.

There was just one thing wrong with the mountain. It was covered with trees, huge tall trees, clear up to the rocky top. There was not room to ride a horse through

the close-set trees, and certainly no room for cattle to graze there, or for grass to grow. Pecos Bill thought and thought, but he could not think of any way to clear the mountain of those trees. He hated to give up and admit there was anything that he could not do. Again and again he rode back to look at the mountain, and try to figure out some way to clear it for his headquarters ranch.

Then one day, imagine his surprise and anger when he found someone else on his mountain! A hundred men were at work at the foot of the mountain putting up a

28

big bunkhouse and a big cookhouse. They did not look like cowboys at all, and they did not have any cattle with them — except for one huge blue-colored ox. He was a hundred times bigger than any steer Pecos Bill had ever seen before, and he ate a whole wagonload of hay at one swallow!

Pecos Bill did not stop to think that he was only one man against a hundred men, and that the huge ox could

kill a man by stepping on him. He rode right up to the camp and asked, 'Who is in charge here?'

'Paul Bunyan,' answered one of the men.

'I want to talk to him,' said Pecos Bill.

The man called, 'Paul,' and there walked out from among the trees the very biggest man in all the world — as big for a man as the Blue Ox was for a steer. Now Pecos Bill himself was a fine figure of a man, six feet two inches high, straight as an arrow and as strong and limber as a rawhide lariat. But this Paul Bunyan was so tall that his knee was higher than Pecos Bill's head! He had a long, dark beard. He wore flat-heeled, broad-toed boots, not like cowboy boots at all. He wore no chaps, and instead of a leather jacket he wore a queer woolen jacket of bright-colored plaid.

But if Pecos Bill was startled, he did not show it. He asked very firmly, 'What are you doing on my mountain?'

'This is my mountain now,' Paul Bunyan announced. 'I've already settled on it.'

'That makes no difference. I laid claim to this land long ago,' Pecos Bill argued.

'Where's the law that says it's yours?' demanded Paul Bunyan.

'Here it is!' exclaimed Pecos Bill. 'This is the law west of the Pecos,' and he laid his hand on his pistol.

'That's not fair!' cried Paul Bunyan. 'I'm not armed. In the North Woods, we don't fight with pistols. We fight with our bare fists or with our axes.'

'Very well,' agreed Pecos Bill. 'I'll give you the choice of weapons. I have no axe, but I'll use my branding iron to hit with.'

Now the branding iron that Pecos Bill carried that day was what is called a running iron. It was only a straight iron bar with a crook on the end of it. Cowboys heat the end of a running iron and draw letters on a steer's hide as you would draw with a piece of crayon on paper.

Pecos Bill heated the end of his branding iron on a blazing star that he had picked up the time the stars fell. He always carried it about with him in his saddle bag, so as to have a fire immediately whenever he needed one. Then the fight started.

Paul Bunyan hit at Pecos Bill so hard with his axe that he cut a huge gash in the earth. People call it the Grand Canyon of the Colorado River now.

Pecos Bill swung his red-hot iron, trying to hit Paul Bunyan, until the sands of the desert were scorched red-colored. That was the beginning of the Painted Desert out in Arizona.

Again Paul Bunyan tried to hit Pecos Bill and hit the

ground instead. The queer rocks that are piled up in the Garden of the Gods in Colorado were split up by Paul Bunyan's axe in that fearful fight.

Pecos Bill's iron, instead of cooling off, got hotter and hotter, until the forests in New Mexico and Arizona were charred. These trees, burnt into stone by the heat from Pecos Bill's running iron, are called Petrified Forests now.

But neither man could get the better of the other. For the first and only time Pecos Bill had met his match. And it was the first and only time that Paul Bunyan's crew had seen a man that could stand up to him.

Finally they both paused to get their breath, and Paul Bunyan suggested, 'Let's sit down and rest a minute.'

'All right,' agreed Pecos Bill, and they sat down on near-by rocks.

As they sat resting, Pecos Bill asked, 'Stranger, why are you so anxious to take my land away from me? Isn't there plenty of other land in the West, that you could have just by laying claim to it?'

'Land!' exclaimed Paul Bunyan. 'It's not the land that I want!'

'Then why are we fighting? What do you want?' inquired the surprised Pecos Bill.

'Why, the trees, of course,' Paul Bunyan explained. 'I'm no rancher. I have no use for land, any longer than it takes to get the timber off. I'll log the trees off that mountain, and then I'll be through with it. I'm a lumber man.'

'Why didn't you say so at first?' exclaimed Pecos Bill.

33

'You are more than welcome to the trees! I've been trying to find some way to get them off the land, so that the grass can grow and my cattle can graze here.'

'They'll be off in a few weeks,' promised Paul Bunyan, and the two men shook hands.

Pecos Bill and Paul Bunyan were good friends after that, each respecting the other for the fight that he had put up. Pecos Bill had his cowboys drive over a herd of nice fat young steers, to furnish beef for Paul Bunyan's loggers while they were clearing off the trees. When Paul Bunyan and his men were through, they left standing their bunkhouse and their cookhouse and the Blue Ox's barn, ready for Pecos Bill's outfit to move in.

Most cattle ranches were not fenced in those days, but Pecos Bill decided to fence his new ranch. He wanted to raise better cattle, that would have more meat and shorter horns on them. To do that, he had to keep his cattle in pastures, and take care of them. That was not easy to do, because Paul Bunyan's men had cut all the wood off the mountain. There was none left even for fence posts.

Pecos Bill solved that problem one cold morning by gathering up a load of Rattlesnakes, stiff and straight as any fence posts. Next, he needed post holes in which to set his fence posts. The post holes would have to be dug all around the ranch, and the cowboys thought they would have a long, hard job digging those holes. But Pecos Bill just went to the nearest Prairie Dog town, and called to the Prairie Dogs in their own language, 'The Rattlesnakes are your worst enemies, are they not? Well, if you'll just dig holes for me to put these Rattlesnakes in, I'll turn them all into fence posts, and they'll never be able to hurt you any more. I'll walk around the mountain, and everywhere I step, you dig a hole.'

The Prairie Dogs gladly followed Pecos Bill and dug a row of holes all the way around the mountain ranch. They dug so fast that in half a day the holes were dug and the fence posts put in them.

'That's fine!' exclaimed Three-Gun Gibbs, Pecos Bill's foreman, when he saw the row of fence posts in place. 'But what are you going to use for a fence?'

'Wire,' explained Pecos Bill. 'We'll stretch wires from post to post.'

'Yes, and the first wild steer that comes along will break right through the fence. Those wires won't stop him any longer than so many strings would. Wires aren't strong enough,' Gibbs argued.

'These wires will stop any animal that breathes!' laughed Pecos Bill. 'See — we'll take cactus thorns and string them along the wires. Then any steers that push against the fence will get pricked sharply by the thorns. They'll let this fence alone!'

Thus Pecos Bill invented the barbed-wire fence, that later was made in huge quantities and used all over the West.

Pecos Bill did such a good job of fencing his ranch that when the Southern Pacific Railroad was built through the West, the contract for fencing the right of way for the railroad was given to him. He did not like to bother his friends the Prairie Dogs again so soon; so this time he called upon his friends the Badgers to dig the holes. He never could teach the Badgers to dig in a straight line, though. That is why the Southern Pacific Railroad winds about on such a crooked track, to this very day. Pecos Bill finally had to fire the Badgers and saw up old dry well holes into two-foot sections, and split them up, to make post holes.

36

PECOS BILL GIVES THE CATTLE DRIVE AND THE RODEO TO THE SOUTHWEST

Pecos bill and his neighbors down in Texas had lots of cattle but not much money. One fall he said to his neighbors, 'Why not round up all the cattle we want to sell, and drive them to Kansas to market?'

They all thought that was a good idea. The cowboys on Pecos Bill's ranches rounded up a million of his cattle to sell, and their neighbors had half a million more to add to the herd. While the cowboys were driving the cattle in to Pecos Bill's headquarters ranch, Pecos Bill and Lightning and Sirius went out and caught ten thousand buffalo, branded them, and drove them in to join the herd of cattle.

37

The great herd had to be driven slowly, never faster than a walk, for hundreds of miles. Pecos Bill was the trail boss, of course. He borrowed from his old friend, Paul Bunyan, the famous Blue Ox, Babe, to be the lead ox of the trail herd. He tied a little bell around Babe's neck, and when Babe stepped out proudly in front of the herd, all the other cattle and the buffalo, too, followed him.

All day the cowboys would drive the cattle slowly on- ward. At night they let the cattle stop to eat and sleep. The men took turns night-herding. The night-herders rode slowly around and around the herd of grazing or sleeping cattle, singing to them, so the cattle would not get scared and stampede and run away into the night. A cowboy named Harry Stephens made this night- herding song:

> Oh, slow up, dogies, quit your roving round,
> You have wandered and tramped all over the ground.
> Oh, graze along, dogies, and feed kinda slow,
> And don't forever be on the go ——
> Oh, move slowly, dogies, move slow.
> Hi — oo, hi — oo, oo — oo.
>
> Oh, lie still, dogies, since you have lain down,
> Stretch away out on the big open ground.

Snore loud, little dogies, and drown the wild sound
That will all go away when the day rolls round —
Lie still, little dogies, lie still.
Hi — oo, hi — oo, oo — oo.

Pecos Bill and his men were driving their herd across unbroken country where they had to make their own trail as they went. There were not any bridges, of course, and when the herd came to a river, the cattle had to wade or swim across. Once they came to a river that was too wide and too deep and too rapid for the cattle to swim. They never would have got across if it had not been for Babe, the Blue Ox. He just drank the river dry, and let them across.

In later years there were many other cattle drives and several famous cattle trails, but no other drive so large as this first one with Pecos Bill as trail boss.

After Pecos Bill and his neighbors had got to Kansas and sold their cattle, they wanted to do something to have some fun. Pecos Bill suggested that they have a rodeo and show the town folks what the cowboys' work is like. It was the first rodeo in all the world. Pecos Bill showed the other cowboys what to do.

The men sat around on the top rail of the corral fence. Dude Hopkins led in a wild pony and held it while Pecos

Bill saddled it and bridled it and jumped on. Then
Hopkins turned him loose, and the pony began to buck.
He jumped forward, backward, to the right and to the
left, up and down, but he could not shake Pecos Bill off
his back. Soon Pecos Bill had the wild pony tamed.

Then he got on Lightning, and showed the crowd
what a real top hand and his top horse can do with
cattle. Slim Morgan turned a wild steer into the corral.
Pecos Bill rode up close, jumped to the ground from the
back of his running horse, and grabbed the steer by the
horns. He threw the steer to the ground, holding it by
the tail and one horn. Cowboys call this 'bull-dogging'
a steer. Pecos Bill was the first cowboy
to do the trick, and he admitted
that he learned it from the
bull-dog Sirius.

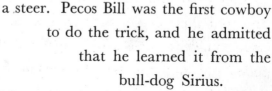

40

Next Pecos Bill showed the crowd how to hog-tie a steer. He threw his lariat around the neck of the running animal, causing it to fall to the ground. Then, while Lightning pulled back on the lariat to keep the steer from getting up, he jumped from his horse and tied the steer's front feet and one hind foot together.

Ever since that time, to this very day, cowboys have been holding rodeos, riding wild horses, bull-dogging steers, and hog-tying them. At rodeos, prizes are given to the cowboys who can do these things best. But no other cowboy has ever been able to ride and rope like Pecos Bill.

From time to time Pecos Bill added to his ranches, until finally they included most of Texas, New Mexico, and Arizona, with parts of Colorado and Montana and Wyoming thrown in. The newer ranches had to be stocked with cattle driven from South Texas.

Young cattle were rounded up and driven over the prairies to their new home. Before the herd was only the great sea of grass. Behind was the trail beaten out by the feet of the cattle as they passed. It was a long, long trail of hundreds of miles, and the little orphan calves, or dogies, got very tired. Sometimes the cowboys had to carry the most weary of the little dogies before them on their horses.

The cattle liked to hear the cowboys singing to them. They felt safer when they could hear the voices of the men who were driving them. This is one of the songs that Pecos Bill made up to sing on the cattle trail:

Whoopee ti yi yo, get along little dogies,
It's your misfortune, and none of my own.
Whoopee ti yi yo, get along little dogies,
For you know that Wyoming will be your new home.

It's whooping and yelling and driving the dogies,
Oh how I wish you would go on.
It's whooping and punching and go on little dogies,
For you know that Wyoming will be your new home.

STRANGERS VISIT
PECOS BILL'S RANCH

AFTER Pecos Bill showed his neighbors how to drive cattle to Kansas and sell them, the cattle men began to make plenty of money. Steers that were worth only five dollars on the range could be sold for fifty dollars in the North.

People all over the world heard how much money Pecos Bill and his neighbors were making. Many of them thought that they would like to come to the West and raise cattle too. Soon men from the northern part of our country and from Canada and England and Scotland and even faraway Australia were turning toward the West. Some of them wanted to be cowboys and work on ranches. Others wanted to buy ranches of their own.

The men from the East knew so little about raising

43

cattle or riding horses that the real cowboys laughed at them and teased them. Pecos Bill always said, though: 'Don't laugh at them, boys. We might look just as funny to people in New York as these tenderfeet do to us. Be kind and polite to them, and give them a chance to learn.'

One day at noon, when Pecos Bill was away from his headquarters ranch, the funniest tenderfoot of all came

44

limping up to the bunk house. He wore a dark brown suit, wrinkled and grayed with sand, and a little brown hat. He had on a high, stiff collar and a fancy necktie, now very dirty and wrinkled. On his upper lip was a black mustache, and his black hair was slicked down with oil.

'Come in, stranger,' invited the foreman, Gibbs, 'and eat dinner with us.'

'Thank you kindly, sir,' the stranger answered, and soon he joined the other men at the noon meal.

Nobody asked him where he was from or why he came West or even what his name was, because those were questions nobody in Pecos Bill's country ever asked a stranger. But the men could hint that they would like to know these things.

'Seems like you've done a lot of walking lately, stranger,' Gibbs remarked.

'Yes,' the stranger agreed, 'I've walked a mighty long way. I've come all the way from Indiana to learn to be

45

a cowboy. Do you suppose Pecos Bill will give me a job on his ranch?'

'That depends,' Gibbs explained, 'on how much you know about cattle and how well you can ride.'

'Oh, I know all about cattle,' the stranger boasted. 'My Pa kept three or four cows all the time on our farm back in Indiana. I've ridden a horse, too. I used to ride our old Dobbin two miles down the road every Saturday night to see my girl.'

'Well, boys, shall we give the stranger a chance to show us how he can ride?' Gibbs asked.

'Sure. I'll rope a nice, gentle horse for him to ride,' Chuck suggested. 'One like Old Paint.'

'Old Paint's the very horse for him,' the cowboys all agreed.

Now Old Paint was an outlaw horse. He had been taken to many rodeos. No cowboy had ever stayed on his back even ten seconds! This was the gentle old horse that the stranger was to ride. He was called a 'paint horse' because he was spotted.

Old Paint looked quiet enough while he was being saddled, and the stranger trustingly climbed on him. Then the fun began. Old Paint reared up, jumped, and kicked. The cowboys expected the innocent stranger to be thrown at the first jump. But the stranger stayed on

46

tight, and did not 'show daylight' between him and the saddle even for a moment. He sat as easily and lightly as if he were in a rocking chair. Then Old Paint made his final effort. He threw himself to the ground, intending to roll on his rider and crush him. But before Old Paint hit the ground, the stranger had jumped lightly out of the saddle, and when Old Paint got to his feet again, the stranger was back in the saddle. In a few moments, the stranger was riding Old Paint around the corral as easily as if this were the gentle old horse that had been promised.

All this time, the cowboys were watching, too surprised to say a word. Finally Chuck gasped, 'We must be dreaming. No man in the world can ride like this, except my brother Bill.'

Just then, the rider stopped Old Paint by the gate of the corral, jumped off, gave the now tame pony a pat, and said in a voice that they all knew very well, 'Well, boys, you can't judge a man by his looks.'

'Pecos Bill!' they cried, so surprised that they hardly knew what to say.

Only once after that, the cowboys met a tenderfoot so ignorant that they felt they just must have some fun with him. He drove out to the ranch in a buggy drawn by a pair of horses. He was a prim little man about sixty

47

years old. Because he wanted to look very Western, he was wearing riding pants, boots, a flannel shirt, and, around his neck, a bright silk handkerchief. He had on a big ten-gallon hat, too. With this outfit, he wore an eyeglass for just one eye, hung from a ribbon around his neck.

'Is Pecos Bill at home?' he asked.

'No, but I'm his foreman,' Gibbs explained.

'I've heard of the big money being made in the cattle business, and I've come to buy a ranch,' he announced. 'Is this one for sale?'

'No, I'm sure Bill wouldn't sell his headquarters ranch. But I could sell you his Rabbit Ears Ranch,' Gibbs suggested.

'Rabbit Ears?' the old gentleman inquired.

'Named for two tall, steep little mountains that stick up like rabbit ears,' explained Gibbs.

'I'll pay cash if the ranch suits me,' the Easterner promised. 'I have the money in gold in a box in the buggy out there.'

'Oh, it will suit you. Best little ranch in the Southwest,' Gibbs lied. 'Twenty thousand acres. Plenty of grass and water for twenty-five hundred cattle.'

48

'Can I buy the cattle, too?' was the next eager question.

'Sure,' Gibbs replied. 'We'll sell for twenty-five dollars a head, and you can get fifty dollars a head for them in Kansas.'

As a matter of fact, the Rabbit Ears Ranch had so little water and such poor grass that Pecos Bill did not have a hundred head of cattle left on it. All the others had been driven off to market. The only ones left were old mossy-horned steers that had hid out in the brush and escaped the roundup.

Three-Gun Gibbs and Dude and Music Mouth and Slim and Chuck all rode toward the Rabbit Ears, with the buyer following in his buggy.

'How are you going to sell him twenty-five hundred cattle when we don't have one hundred there?' the others asked Gibbs.

'You wait and see,' was the only answer he would make.

When they got to the ranch, the Easterner rested while

the cowboys rode out to find the steers and drive them in. The old mossy horns were still so hard to find that the cowboys came back toward their camp driving only twenty-five steers before them. That did not worry Gibbs any, though. He had the buyer stand at the foot of one of the Rabbit Ears while a bunch of twenty-five cattle were driven by and counted.

In a few minutes twenty-five more came around the curve in the trail, and then a few minutes later twenty-five more were counted. The buyer never did realize that the same bunch of cattle were being driven around and around the mountain and made to pass in front of him a hundred times. He only said, 'Fancy dividing them into groups of twenty-five! Neat, I call that!'

The Easterner bought twenty-five steers, but paid for twenty-five hundred! He paid twenty-five dollars a head when five dollars would have bought a good steer! And he got tough old mossy horns that he could not sell to somebody else at any price! Besides that, he had bought a ranch where he could not raise anything but sagebrush.

The cowboys laughed all the way home about the joke that they had played. When they told Pecos Bill, he laughed, too, but he made them return the Easterner's money.

PECOS BILL TAMES
THE CATTLE RUSTLERS

O<small>NE</small> of the best things that Pecos Bill did for the cattle country was to get rid of the cattle and horse thieves. A gang of them had their hang-out on Mystery Mountain. They were called Alkali's Gang because their leader was an outlaw named Alkali Ike. They stole horses and cattle from all the neighboring ranches and sold them. They had shot several cowboys who tried to protect stock from being stolen. One night they stole a herd of ꟻB cattle, and shot the night-herder. Wounded as he was, he clung to his horse, and galloped to the headquarters ranch to report the theft to Pecos Bill and the cowboys of the ꟻB outfit.

They all pulled on their boots and reached for their guns (except Three-Gun Gibbs, who even slept in his).

In a moment the cowboys were ready to jump on their horses and rush to Mystery Mountain to revenge their comrade. But Pecos Bill said: 'Not this way, boys. They would kill several of us while we were killing them. I must go alone, and surprise them. There must be no lives lost.'

The cowboys all begged to go with him, but Pecos

Bill said: 'No, I go alone. But you follow me to the foot of the mountain, and if you hear shooting at their camp, you ride in to help me.'

He rode Lightning up the mountain to within a mile of the outlaw's camp. There he left Lightning (dropping the bridle reins to the ground, as cowboys do, instead of tying them to something). Taking with him his lariat and his six-shooter, he crept toward the camp. He reached it just before daybreak, while the outlaws were eating their breakfast. They squatted around their campfire, satisfied with their night's work and quite unaware that they had been followed. Beyond their camp, Pecos Bill could

see his herd of fine young short-horn cattle, milling around in a crude corral. Suddenly he stepped forward out of the darkness into the circle of firelight, holding the pistol in his hand.

'Put 'em up, boys,' he snapped.

Slowly and reluctantly, the outlaws raised their hands above their heads — all except their leader, Alkali Ike. Alkali pulled his pistol out and began to shoot at Pecos Bill. But Pecos Bill dodged so fast that not one of the bullets hit him. He fired just one shot, and his bullet cut off the trigger finger of Alkali's right hand. Cursing, Alkali raised his hands, too.

The sound of the shooting brought Pecos Bill's cowboys to his assistance, as fast as their horses could run up the mountain trail. 'Take the guns off these prisoners,' he directed.

Then he threw his lariat around the waist of the outlaws, tying them all up together. Handing the end of the lariat to his foreman, Three-Gun Gibbs, he ordered, 'Lead them to the border and kick them over.'

None of Alkali's gang ever came back, they were so afraid of Pecos Bill.

54

PECOS BILL LETS
THE WEATHER ALONE

Pecos bill was a most industrious man. When he was not busy inventing important things, like short-horn cattle and barbed-wire fences and windmills, he kept busy putting little humorous touches on things. It was Pecos Bill that put the horns on horned toads. He invented the tumbleweeds, too, that roll so merrily and wildly across the plains in the fall, like a herd of cattle stampeding.

The only thing Pecos Bill could not do much to improve was the weather. Perhaps he never seriously tried to do anything about the weather, because he was a man that liked plenty of change and excitement, and the weather in the Southwest can be depended upon for that. Pecos Bill used to say that only newcomers or natural-born fools try to predict the weather in Texas.

An experience that Pecos Bill had one time when he went swimming shows how much change and excitement the weather in the Southwest can provide. One warm, cloudy fall day he thought he would go swimming. He went down to the river, undressed, and jumped off the river bank, thinking that he would dive into the nice, deep hole of water just below. While he was jumping, though, a drought came along and dried up all the water. For a moment it looked as if Pecos Bill would land on the rocks of the river bed, and bring his glorious career to an untimely end. But luckily, before he hit the rocks, a flood came up, and filled the river again. Still, his troubles were not over, because just as he came to the surface after his dive, a norther blew up and froze him into the ice. He would have frozen to death if the sun had not come out just then and melted the ice.

Yes, there is generally plenty of change in the weather in Pecos Bill's country. One winter, though, the cold spell lasted two weeks, and ever since then the old-

timers have talked about 'the year of the big freeze.'
The blizzard hit suddenly, as usual. Pecos Bill had
ridden into Fort Worth to do some trading. He was
riding Lightning, of course, and Sirius was trotting behind at Lightning's heels. It was a warm, sunny day,
almost as warm as summer. The store was crowded with
cowboys. One of them happened to glance out of the
window, and shouted a warning to the others,

'Look! a Blue Norther!'

Sure enough, a small blue-black cloud was visible, far
away on the horizon. The cowboys all rushed for their
horses and rode toward home as fast as they could go.
The blue-black cloud got bigger and bigger until it
covered all the sky. The wind blew bitter cold, and rain

and sleet began to fall. Lightning ran so fast, though, that Pecos Bill was able to keep just on the edge of the blizzard. When they got to the ranch house, Lightning's forequarters were lathered white with sweat and steaming with heat, but his hindquarters were covered with ice! As for Sirius, he had to swim all the way home, because Pecos Bill rode on the edge of the blizzard, with the rain falling in torrents just behind him. Sirius swam along behind Lightning, with the sleet and ice clinging to his hair.

The ʙ cowboys feasted on roast duck and fried frogs' legs and fried fish during that cold spell. The ducks were frozen on the lake before they could fly away, the norther struck so suddenly. The bull frogs saw the blue cloud coming and jumped into the water, but then they stuck their heads out again to see the norther strike, and got their heads frozen in the ice. The ice over the lake was sprinkled with frogs' heads and with ducks, so all the cowboys had to do was to dig them out and carry them home, still frozen. The fish were even easier to pick up, for they were just scattered around on top of the ice. The water was so hot, just before the blizzard struck, that the fish jumped out of the water for a breath of cool air, and were frozen in midair, falling back on the newly formed ice.

The cowboys could have caught the fish and frogs, though, even if they had been under the ice — thanks to the foresight of Pecos Bill. While the weather was still warm, he had taken his post-hole auger and bored holes in the water. Of course, when the water froze, the holes were left frozen in the ice.

Pecos Bill did not lose many cattle during the big freeze. The cowboys drove the herd into a sheltered canyon for protection from the wind. Even in there, it was so cold that the cowboys could not hear the bellowing of the cattle or each others' voices — the sounds had all frozen. When the thaw came, the noise from that canyon was deafening. For miles around people heard men yelling and cattle bawling, as the sounds melted.

Pecos Bill was always the one to blow out the light in the bunkhouse at bedtime, because he moved so quickly that he could blow out the flame and then kick off his boots and jump in bed before the room got dark. During the big freeze, though, when he tried to blow out the light, he found that the flame was frozen. He had to thaw it out by the fire before he could blow it out.

In Amarillo, though, people did not have to bother about a light at night during those two weeks. The sun came out, the second day of the freeze, and the sunshine itself got frozen. All the chickens died for want of sleep. They thought it was daylight all the time, of course, and never did go to bed.

There were sometimes dust storms, too, in Pecos Bill's country. During a dust storm, the wind would blow hard for several hours, scoop up sand from the plains, carry it through the air, and finally drop it somewhere else. During the storm, the air was full of dirt, and the sky as dark as at night. Sometimes a cowboy could hardly see as far as his cowpony's nose, even at noon. These dust storms made the most surprising changes in the landscape. One time, before a storm, Pecos Bill saw a little bush on the top of a certain hill. After the storm, the hill was not there at all, and the bush was a tree one hundred feet tall! It had been a tall tree all the time, of course, but had been almost entirely covered by sand, blown over it by some past storm and now blown away by the recent storm.

Pecos Bill used to see Prairie Dog holes sticking up fifty feet in the air after a dust storm had blown the sand from around them. Post holes were left sticking up in the air that way, too, sometimes.

60

PECOS BILL'S TRUE LOVE

ALL the girls liked Pecos Bill, and he laughed
and danced with them all. But he never cared very much
for any of them until one day he met Sue. The first time
he saw her she was riding down the river on a catfish as
big as a whale. She was so pretty and sweet and happy-
looking and rode so well that Pecos Bill fell in love with
her at first sight. Soon he found that she danced as well
as she rode. In fact, she was called Lightfoot Sue, because she was so light on her feet and could turn so
rapidly in the whirl of the dance. More than that, Sue
could cook! The dinners she cooked for Pecos Bill, when
he came to see her, made the meals poor old Beans
cooked out on the range taste like feed for cattle.

Soon, Pecos Bill asked her to marry him. But she
answered: 'I appreciate the honor you do me in asking

61

me to become your wife. But we haven't known each other very long. How can we be sure we love each other? Maybe you just think you love me, because you like the way I ride and dance and cook.'

'No, Sue,' Pecos Bill cried, 'I love you truly because you are sweet and good, and I would love you just as much if you couldn't ride or dance, or even cook.'

'Then prove your love for me,' Sue demanded. 'Let me ride your Lightning horse. Nobody but you ever gets on him, and if you'll let me ride him, I'll know that you really love me.'

'But, Sue,' Bill protested, 'you don't know what you're asking. Lightning would throw you, and you might be hurt badly. I couldn't let you run that risk. Ask me to do anything else for you, but don't ask me to lend you Lightning.'

'I know now you don't love me,' Sue wept. 'I don't ever want to see you again!'

Poor Pecos Bill could not bear to hear Sue talk like that, or to see her cry; so he finally gave in, much against his best judgment. 'Well, honey,' he said, 'on our wedding day, you can ride Lightning.'

He really thought that before their wedding day, he could talk her out of the idea. But she continued to insist that, before she married him, she must test his love.

The fateful day dawned clear and bright. Neighbors for hundreds of miles around had ridden in for the wedding, and the preacher was ready for the ceremony.

'Bill, you promised I could ride Lightning today,' Sue reminded him.

Afraid for the first time in his life, afraid for Sue, Pecos Bill walked sadly with her to the corral where Lightning was waiting. Slowly he saddled his horse, and buckled the halter that Lightning wore instead of a bridle. Sue's father and mother were begging her to change her mind, and the friends that crowded around the gate of the corral added their protests. But all failed to persuade her. With a toss of her pretty head, she blew a kiss to the watching crowd, and jumped on Lightning's back.

Immediately Lightning began to jump and buck. For only a moment was Sue able to stay in the saddle. Then off she flew, and up, up, up, into the air. She was thrown so hard and so far that she went clear up to the moon, and stuck there. Her parents begged Pecos Bill to rope her and pull her down, but she was afraid to fall so far and would not let him rope her. You can see her in the moon to this day. Look closely when the moon is full, and you will see her there. Sometimes you see her full figure, facing toward your right, bent over in a

despairing attitude, as she must have looked when she first was thrown to the moon. Again, sometimes you see just her head, facing toward your left, and she looks happier and more alive, as if she has got used to living in the moon.

But Pecos Bill could never be comforted for his loss.

64

He blamed himself for letting Sue get on Lightning, and he was heartbroken because he had lost her. He cried so that his tears made the Salt River in Arizona.

ADIOS, PECOS BILL

Pecos bill felt very sad after he lost Sue. He gazed longingly up at her at night, up in the moon, and wished that he could join her. The West was no longer what it used to be. Many of the ranches had been cut into farms. The country was too closely settled, the old-time cattle men and cowboys thought.

Nobody sees Pecos Bill these days, in Cheyenne or Phoenix or Santa Fe or any of his old trading posts. Nobody seems to know just where he is. Some say that he is dead. But that cannot be true, because whenever you talk to a real, old-fashioned cattle man, you hear more stories of Pecos Bill. He must be alive somewhere, still doing the glorious deeds that cowboys love to tell, and adding more and more stories to the brave legend of Pecos Bill.

Some say that he has found the Lost Canyon, and there established a new and better ranch, with Chuck and Slim and Dude and Music Mouth and Three-Gun Gibbs and all the rest of his old outfit. In Lost Canyon, he is safely away from the farmers who have broken up the ranch country and from the new-style cowboys that ride automobiles instead of broncos.

Perhaps the truth of the matter is that Pecos Bill is alive now, and always will be alive, just where he always has been — in the hearts of the cowboys who find relief from their toil and care in telling of a gay, fearless hero who braves all toil and care with ready laughter on his lips and a twinkle in his eye.

Wherever Pecos Bill may be, the time has come to say, in the language of the Mexican cowboys of the border:

'Adios, hasta la vista, Pecos Bill!'

68

9964 2